THE BOY WITH THE OLD GUITAR

Cover design by Julian Loveday.
All drawings by John Loveday.

THE BOY WITH THE OLD GUITAR

AND OTHER POEMS

including

CITY OF FLOWERS

John Loveday

Matador
Unit E2 Airfield Business Park,
Harrison Road, Market Harborough,
Leicestershire. LE16 7UL
Tel: 0116 2792299
Email: books@troubador.co.uk
Web: www.troubador.co.uk/matador
Twitter: @matadorbooks

ISBN 978 1803135 397

British Library Cataloguing in Publication Data.
A catalogue record for this book is available from the British Library.

Printed and bound in Great Britain by 4edge Limited
Typeset in 13pt Adobe Garamond Pro by Troubador Publishing Ltd, Leicester, UK

Matador is an imprint of Troubador Publishing Ltd

To Sharon and Julian
and to the memory of Marina

I chose the title-poem for its simple, believable story. The rest accrued in the usual way.

John Loveday

CONTENTS

THE BOY WITH THE OLD GUITAR

They left him out from all they did –
Not meaning to, careless of hurt,
His wide, sad eyes, that watched the fun,
Left on the edge, not in with them –
Aside always, a boy apart.

A lady found an old guitar,
Gave it to him. He bent his neck,
Looked down and strummed. It sounded weird,
They fell about, but jealousy
Was never far from what they felt.

He moved away. They didn't know
Till he had gone, then someone said.
Much later on, they heard that he
Had learned to play the old guitar
So very well. It wasn't true,

It couldn't be, they all agreed.
They laughed, and thought of that first time
They fell about. Later, they heard
That he was in a proper band.
He wrote a song. They heard it sung.

Then he was on 'Top of the Pops',
And they all said that he grew up
With them, their friend. They told about
The old guitar, how he 'played good'.
They knew that they left something out.

The years went by. One summer night
Two of them stood for tickets in
A hopeful queue. The line was long.
A small group of musicians passed.
One paused, looked round. His eyes met theirs.

Then he walked on. Their thoughts were back
With that weird sound from long ago.
They were about to give up, when
A girl came out and asked their names.
'You're special guests,' she said. 'Come in.'

There was a note. It said, *'I knew*
You straight away. Two seats, and see
you afterwards'. There is no need
To tell you how he played that night.
Some say it's part of history.

They only knew, when he stood there,
It seemed as if he played into
Another time and back again
To where they stood and cheered and cried
Until the night's last echo died.

They found him quiet, the boy apart.
'My luck, no doubt, in seeing you.
I played my best. So glad you came.
It's good to know you wanted to,
And I could see you weren't left out.'

He reached, took up a battered case
And opened it. 'It goes where I
Go – always will. I played it once
Tonight, for you.' They said they knew.

HENRY MOORE
FETCHES APPLES

The cellar steps are dark,
The boy goes nervously
To fetch the apples up
His mother bakes for tea.

His feet side-turned for flight,
He keeps an eye on where
The shape of daylight shows
Behind him on the stair.

Years afterwards, he'll say
Those holes he carved in stone
Became *ways out to light*
Like that remembered one

RACHEL SITS

'… a little Jewish girl of thirteen
years or so with red hair'
                    – WR Sickert, 1907

Mister Sickert comes in.
'At the looking-glass,'
He says. 'Look in there.'

I look at my face,
At his face behind,
His long stare,

Then the top of his head
As he starts to draw.
In the hush, I can hear

The touch of his pencil,
Soft, soft, soft.
He is drawing my hair,

Now, *softer*, my face.
I look in there
To see what he sees.

He smiles back at me.
O, my red hair,
My red hair.

(In the summer of 1907, Sickert made six paintings
of 'Little Rachel' in his first-floor rented room at
6 Mornington Crescent, NW1.)

BETTY DROWNING

Her dress floated out on the water,
Her dark curls spread too,
I caught her hair and held her,
And did not let her go.

She kisses me, says I saved her,
So I do not tell her no,
I cannot, cannot remember
That day sixty years ago.

THE BOY LOOKED OUT

The boy looked out from a doorway,
Up to the pasture where
The white horse stood in sunlight,
And thought he saw Burkhart there,
Who had died from an Indian arrow
Three days before.

Troubled, the boy came to Bessie,
Who had raised him, loved and fed,
And told of the horse in sunlight,
Of how he'd seen Burkhart, not dead.
Gently, 'We have to be able
To believe things like that,' Bessie said.

WHEN THE OTHERS HAD GONE

When the others had gone
We wanted to stay.
You said you should go
But you didn't go.

The shadows grew longer over the ground,
We talked a bit, we fooled around.
You said you should go
But you didn't go.

We looked at each other,
We looked away.
You said you should go
But you didn't go.

I should have gone
But I wanted to stay.

BOY WAITING

Waiting for you under wet trees.
Perhaps you won't come.
Perhaps you never intended to from the start.

Next time I see you it will be so easy.
You'll give some excuse that will seem so true.
I won't be able to show I don't believe you,

Because I'd wait for you somewhere again if I could,
Pretending you might come – and perhaps you would.

NIGHT TRAIN

The sound of a train from far away
Came through my window,
And happy voices I thought I knew
Came in snatches –

Then one was you.

MARINA

The sun is shining
And the sky is blue,
You wrote when five years old,
A good start to a story,
Always used – until the teacher said,
'Write something new.'
You did: *The sky is blue*
And the sun is shining.
So they were,
Where your thoughts grew.

However turned, the words stay true
To how the world seemed then to you:
The sun is shining
And the sky is blue

THE ROCKING-HORSE'S TAIL

The child is alone in the room.
She is running her hands through the hair
Of the rocking-horse's tail,
A flow of silky light,
So soft, believable,
A wondrous feel of the real
Hair of a living horse,
As once this was –
Her tenderness a spell
To hold all loveliness close there?
Future moments she can't foretell,
Or remembered hands, touching her hair?

IN SULHAM WOODS
(C.1986)

For Cron

Your hands near mine on the handlebar,
Seat on the crossbar, safe, my arms
Protecting: this is how we ride
In Sulham Woods, our favourite paths,
Where love and wonderment abound,
Sunlight dazzles through the leaves,
And, what you love to know the most,
The dogs are barking up wrong trees.

CHILD IN SUNLIGHT

Child in sunlight, by the Sunday river,
A white cotton hat shielding two-year eyes,
I would record, if I could, for ever,
In fluent brush-strokes, each nuance and shimmer
Of this moment in sunlight you will not remember.

ME AND YOU

A little white horse stands in the meadow.
The grasses are long, almost touching his belly.

The white tail swishes at bothering flies,
The white mane tosses. One step, two.
We stand watching, just me and you.

THE MAN FROM
THE WAR

Mr George Kettle came home from the war
With a wooden leg he didn't have before.

He counted his shillings and bought a shed
Just big enough to sit in to earn his bread.

He fixed a bench by the window's light,
Mended boots and shoes from morning till light,

Six days of the week, perched on his stool,
Hammering, stitching, nobody's fool,

His door wide open, so everyone saw
George on his stool, and came to the door.

He liked to listen. They liked to stand
Talking with George at his busy right hand.

His dark eyes welcomed, his handsome face smiled
When I came with my shoes when I was a child.

MAKE MY DAY

He rides in from hillside or prairie,
From where no-one can say,
To someplace where someone will need him,
His three words, 'Make my day'

He spoke them in one scene only,
But now they will always stay,
Chilling the screen, though unspoken,
His three words, 'Make my day'

The crook with the gun will falter,
The cowards will sidle away,
And no girl at the end can alter
His three words, 'Make my day'

WHERE BILLY WAS

Stayed there alone the whole afternoon.
Nobody came there. It wasn't good grass,
Just old dry grass, dead mostly, tall.
Not saying where. Could've been anywhere.
You'll never find it. Don't mind if you do.
You wouldn't know it if you found it.
There's nothing to see, just old dry grass.
Just stayed there, that's all;
Where nobody could see,
And I couldn't see nobody,
And didn't want to.
Sparrers flew over. One shit on me.

A titchy field-mouse came, sat looking up.
I sat so still, thought my heart could stop.

TINKER, TAILOR

Tinker, tailor, soldier, sailor/This year, next year, sometime…
Traditional children's chants.

Prune stone, damson, greengage, plum –
All foretold what we'd become.

Plum stone, greengage, damson, prune –
Touched again, they told how soon.

We believed them, in a way,
Though the forecasts changed each day.

Fruitful summers prophesied,
Plums and custard lied and lied,

Years and years of changing fates
Strewn around our dinner plates.

SNOW

The snow, the snow is falling, snow,
Snow, snow, on everything, on me,
My face turned up, my eyelids, lips,
My nose. Now open eyes.

Across the Green there's nothing
Anymore, no trees the other side,
No paths, no goalposts, no one there.
Turning: the oak tree halfway up
Beside the road that disappears,
The willows further left, the ash,
Just there enough to see: someone
Would be a ghost. A moving light,
Two lights come through, bigger, bigger,
But slowly. He can't see, comes down,
And past, and gone, and silently
Almost. The fire indoors: go in.
'Come in,' she's telling me.

LANDSCAPE

Henry Moore rubs his mother's back
To ease her pain: the boy's hands meet and part,
And find, unknowingly, upon those slopes,
The landscape of his future art.

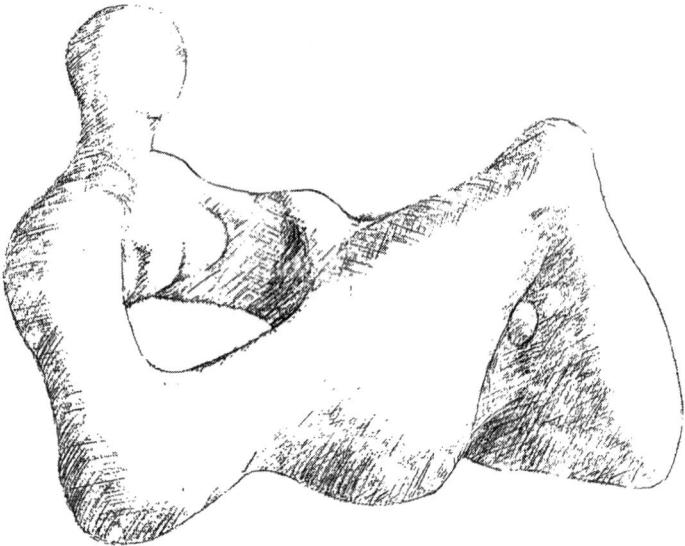

ROY
(b.1902, d.1910)

(on a pen and ink drawing, c 1907, made
when the artist was fifteen/sixteen)

Just being there, small boy against
A low, dark-boarded pew his arm
Could rest elbow-to-shoulder on,
The way they did, forearm along
A bit, hand down the other side.
His face is looking out, away.

What Stanley was drawing here would be,
So soon, dear memory: Roy's cheek,
An ear, light rough-cut hair, his suit,
Socks slipping down, his shoes drawn small,
Legs smaller than they should have been.

So this is all. He did not come
With others rising on that day
In Cookham churchyard. Close to home,
A child, he could not find his way.

THE FOREST HAS DANGERS

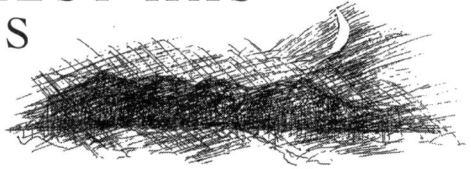

'There's a road through the forest,' the old woman said,
'But don't go there tonight.' He asked why not.
'The forest has dangers, boy. Sleep in my bed.'

His heart turned over. He murmured that he
Must travel on, then saw his mistake.
'I'm sorry, boy, I meant you could be

Safe here in my inn till the morning light.'
But he said he would go. She said, 'God's speed.'
He turned back once, nearly out of sight.

A girl was waving. The old one had gone.
He raised his hand, and the girl seemed to call.
He longed to return, but his road was on.

The girl was waving as if she had stood
There all the while and he had not seen.
Then darkness fell as he entered the wood.

THE BOATMAN'S STORY

For a few days in late July 1815, Napoleon waited aboard HMS Bellerophon, in hope of being granted asylum in England.

The day I saw Napoleon
Was when that great ship came
And lay off Plymouth harbour bar
And someone called my name

Because the great Napoleon
Was there for all to see
If they could find a goodly man
With a goodly boat, like me.

I rowed them to Napoleon
Who stood there, aft, so small,
With all his empires lost and gone,
His soldiers gone an' all.

It was a sad Napoleon
We came to see that day
But little boats in hundreds came,
Then drifted, slow, away.

The flowers for Napoleon
They floated on the wave
And it was strange our enemy
Should see the flowers we gave.

The day I saw Napoleon
A girl with flowers stood tall,
I touched her back to steady her,
Up there he heard her call.

She saw the great Napoleon,
He raised his hat so high,
It seemed a moment's happiness –
She turned to me to cry.

So when we left Napoleon
My joy raced on and on,
I tied my boat, turned to the girl,
But, in the crowd, she'd gone.

PLAY THIS AGAIN, LOVE

A response to 'Beau Sejour,
a jazz composition by Pete Allen

Play this again, love,
Wherever you are –
There's no place too lonely,
There's no place too far
For you to remember
How once we were –
And those who remember
The light of your star.

Play this again, love,
For the days that were free –
In forest or desert,
On mountain or sea.
Play this again, love,
Just once more for me –
Tell all the strangers
How we used to be.

Play this again, love,
Play this once more –
Say the roads are all lonely
That lead from this shore,
But they will be taken,
They've been taken before –
A door's there to open:
You open the door.

Play this again, love,
Wherever you are –
There's no place too lonely,
There's no place too far

NOTHING STAYS SPECIAL

A Country Song Lyric

'Nothing stays special for long,' he said,
'But I'd like to be special for you.'
She loved what he said as he stood by her bed,
But she knew he'd not make it be true.

He rode away. He looked back but twice.
He was thinking of words from the past:
'A good woman is … a pearl of great price.'
But he thought, 'And the special don't last.'

He rode on, restless, ever on West.
Men whose names are legend he knew.
So, seven years went, in the ways of the West,
But the pearls of great price, they were few.

Then, on a day when his horse turned away
From the path he had set it upon,
He let it go, heedless: 'Oh, hell, come what may!'
But by sundown, he knew the way on.

She with a hand on his son's gold head
Was an image his dreaming had made.
'Some things that are special, stay special,' she said.
He told how his dreams had stayed.

No map now marks any place with a word
Where they lived in a bygone day,
But 'Pearl Place' is a name some locals heard
For where a few ruins lay,

For where a few ruins lay.

*The song is available on all usual channels for
download and can be heard on*:
www.johnloveday.net
Lyric – John Loveday.
Vocals and Music – Jan S. Robinson

A FLAME IN FIESOLE

… CHE IL 12 AGUSTO 1944
DIEDERO LA VITA PER SALVARE
INNOCENTI OSTAGGI
(From a memorial to three carabinieri)

A mound below a high stone wall;
Three spare-limbed olive trees—though young,
Already gnarled; below the mound,
Another wall, the path on which we stand;
An iron rail; the fall
Of terraces to Florence, pearled
In August haze.
We pause.
A jagged flame is poised in bronze
Among the little olives, stark,
Half-abstract, dominant. It soars
Across our vision, silhouette
Almost, against the sunlit stone,
The sky's blue angularities.
Move round. Sharp sides assume their grey:

Dark forks that frame pale olive-blur,
Parched grass, the tips of cypresses,
Diminishing. Climb to the mound.
Forked grey becomes green patina,
Each leaping shape defined on sky
Or Tuscany. The fourth side shows,
Beyond a group of trees, a road,
The way we came, they would have come,
The executioners.
Today,
A small truck comes, a man in shorts,
Straw hat, two carabinieri—boys
Of half his age. They'll help him lay
Fresh turf across the baring mound.
They go, to take off uniform.
He walks about, surveys. I ask
If he speaks English. "No", he laughs,
And jabbers on, but tries to cross
The barrier, holds out his hand
Towards the hazy hills, the spread
Of Florence shimmering…
"Che bella citta!" Understand?
More than he knows. Now we converse
By guesswork, sign, as children do.

I indicate the sculpture's plaque,
The three men's names, the words I drew
Some meaning from last year,
Diedero la vita per
Salvare innocenti ostaggi.
I raise an unseen rifle, aim,
But he corrects me, rakes the wall
With sharp dry-throated broken rasps,
Hands grasped on shuddering phantom steel,
Close to his belly, arcing round,
Abruptly done. "Dodici Agusto…
Domani… anniversario…"
Tomorrow they will come… "polizia…
Armi… il Generate…"—all.
I see them moving through the trees
And gathering. His hands spread turf
In gesture, as the boys return
In shorts and track-shoes, golden-skinned.
They pass the rolled turf up to him.
He spreads, along the mound's edge, quick
And competent—a gardener by trade?
The communale handyman?
The cimitero keeper? Graves
Would have made him humorous. His laugh
And jabber set the tone, belie
The sadness that inheres; the sun

Also—it would have dazzled them,
Scorched this high wall, burned on the gun,
Blotched sweat on backs of uniforms…
Lightly, a woman calls
Some comment down. The man responds,
Their interchange is jocular—
It could be coarse. More women come
Beside her as she talks, look down.
Working, he straddles wide, his balls
Are classic Florentine. I snap
Him from below, behind—the turn
To take a turf, the bend to spread,
The lithe boys reaching up, the flame
Reared overhead. The past stands off,
Grey-clad among the trees,
Its motorcycles throb unheard,
Its helmets, side-cars, guns unseen.
The grass, green memory, ascends.
Across the rail a young man's name,
A girl's, are scrawled in fibre-tip,
A happy, boastful verb between.

*A FLAME IN FIESOLE was originally published
in ENCOUNTER magazine (1987)*

BLUE BAR GARDEN, FIESOLE

Mid-afternoon in the Blue Bar garden
Beneath a roof of vines sun speckles through
To tablecloths and chairs, all blue,
Receding to blue railings, dark
Against leaves' luminosity.
Few customers. A desultory waiter
Comes and goes. The further corner, in the sun,
Draws three young men, a girl. Germans, perhaps.
Their blond hair haloes there. The men
Strip off their shirts; the girl, dark-singleted,
Puts up her long legs to a chair
And pulls her pink skirt high.

On such an August afternoon,
The leutnant Hiesserich was grim,
Interrogation yielding nil. Shoot them!'
By then, the evening. The escort came
Into the house next door, Hotel Aurora;
After a while, went out behind.
The hostages said how they heard
The crackle of automatic weapon fire –
'A first, a second burst, some pistol shots.'

MEMO

Gratitude to those who taught me love,
Disdain for those who taught me fear,
Affection for those who taught me truth:
Those fading faces of yesteryear.

THE END

Get out of this poem,
Leave it empty,
Without a word.
Someone could use the page,
Fill it with their pleasure,
Pain, or whatever, whatever…
Stand aside;
One of your readers has something to say.
He? She?
Walk off the stage,
Just slip away

CITY OF FLOWERS

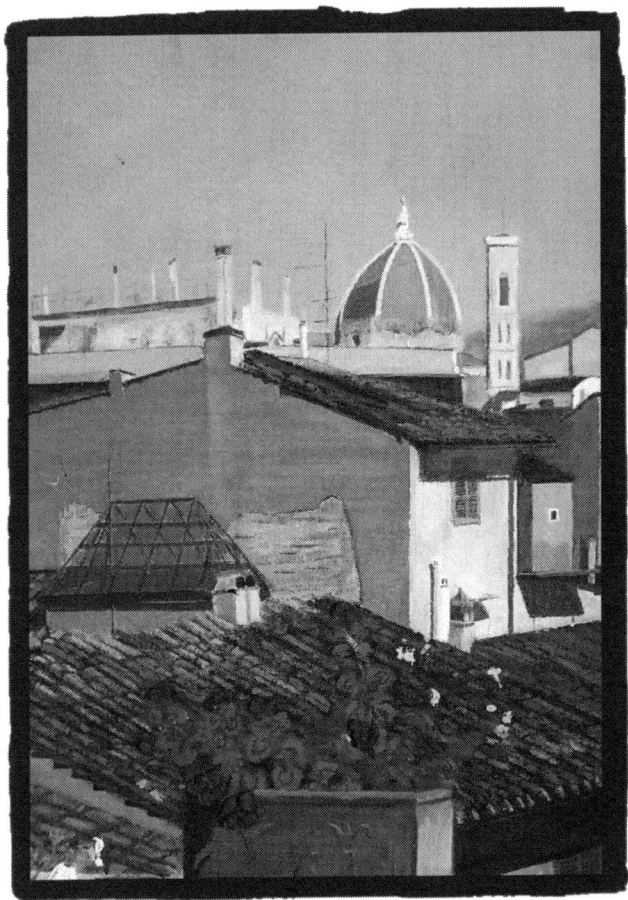

INTERIOR, FLORENCE

Behind which green shutters do you stand,
Girl at the long mirror, in a room's dim light,
Regarding yourself? holding one hand
To a pearly areola, not touching quite,
The other in shadow, feet casually apart,
Stayed by your image at the wardrobe door,
Framed for a moment, not thinking of art,
Botticellis or Titians, your clothes on the floor,
But asking, as if for the first time, with surprise,
'Am I beautiful?' your eyes now asking a stranger's eyes

THE FLOWER BOX

*(detail from an oil painting
of a Florentine roof-garden)*

Where two walls met, upon the lower one
A terra-cotta box for flowers stood, set
A little 'out of true'. August: near-blue
Sharp-angled shadows on the terrace floor,
Between, below, white garden furniture.
The walls gleamed white; beyond, two conifers
Stood in small flowers, their trunks slight curves
Rising to mottled darknesses, above blue hills,
The inlaid roofscape's domes and towers.
The picture framed and hung, lived-with a year,
The box seemed sometimes to confuse: the eye,
Across a room, construed perspective wrong,
A wall seemed oddly turned. The art, to know
What to leave out ... It had to go:
I covered it with green, a blur of bloom.
No one could know it ever there,
As if some handyman had shifted it

To stand among those others on the floor.
Two centuries, and some sharp eye will stare
Into a patch of green transparency,
See what I hid, and wonder why,
Be moved by its slow emergence there.

THE FLOWER BOX was originally published in
ENCOUNTER magazine (1989)

THE PEEKING SISTER

She is peeking,
Chit of ten, or younger,
From behind a hedge,
At a girl suckling a baby
As she stands on a pathway,
On a day long enough ago
For the print to be in sepia
And both girls dead,
Like the man who photographed them,
Sisters, perhaps, a few Tuscan summers
And a hedge between them,
The little one peeking
In a dream of motherhood,
Her sister inhabiting
Another part of the same dream,
Knowing, wiser, but still delighting,

Still astounded at the mystery
Of the globe in her hand,
Little madonna,
Madonna of Sepia,
Of Alinari, photographer,
Little Madonna of the Peeking Sister.